SNOW FROM THE NORTH

By the same author

A Country on Fire, Littlewood Press 1986
A Halifax Cider Jar, Yorkshire Art Circus 1987
Into the Ashes, Littlewood Press 1988
Sky Burial, Dangaroo Press 1989

Snow from the North

Graham Mort

Dangaroo Press

ACKNOWLEDGEMENTS:

Acknowledgements are due to the following:

The Green Book, Iron, Poetry Wales, The North, Acumen, Outposts, The New Welsh Review, BBC Radio 3 'New Voices', *Stand, The Observer Review, Lines Review, Westwords, The Echo Room, Yorkshire Artscene, Orbis, Kunapipi*.

Yorkshire & Humberside
A R T S

'Storm In Suburbia' has appeared in *Iron*.

'The Fall' has appeared in *Poetry Wales*

'The Red Field' was derived from the Paul Klee painting 'Ins Nachbarhaus' It won a Duncan Lawrie prize in the 1992 Arvon Foundation International Poetry Competition.

Thanks to Caroline Forbes for permission to reproduce her photograph of the author.

Thanks to Janet Sampson for 'Snow from the North' which was painted especially for the cover of the book.

This book is copyright. Apart from any fair dealing for the purpose of private study, criticism or review, as permitted under the Copyright Act, no part may be reproduced by any process without written permission. Enquiries should be made to the publisher.

© Graham Mort 1992

First published in 1992 by Dangaroo Press
Australia: G.P.O. Box 1209, Sydney, New South Wales, 2001
Denmark: Pinds Hus, Geding Søvej 21, 8381 Mundelstrup
UK: 80 Kensington Road, Earlsdon, Coventry. CV5 6GH

ISBN 1 871049 92 X
Printed in Great Britain by Villiers Publications, London N6

For Maggie

For Maggie

CONTENTS

Amnesiac	9
A Mercenary Soldier Turns for Home	11
Snow from the North	13
Drowning at Pouzauges	14
Photographic Memory	16
Night Ride: BMW R/80	17
A Year of Dust	18
Mother and Son	19
Frost	21
M6 Services	22
Unemployed: Tranmere 1991	23
Miss Devlin at the Sea View Hotel	25
Passing Out	28
Mole Totem	30
Home in April	31
Climbing With a Dead Man	32
Above Grasmere	34
Storm in Suburbia	36
Mushrooming	49
Mending his Motorcycle in Wartime	51
Family Reunion	53
Kill	56
Guy Fawkes' Night	58
The Fall	59
On Caton Road	64
Boy With Dead Mole	66
An Irish Bishop in Peru	68
Invasion	70
Anfal	72
Webs	74
A Matchstick Model of the Forth Bridge	76
An Eel at Lake Coniston	78
The Red Field	82

Amnesiac

The mirror shows me a map of skin
Without reference points:
I have seen other men like him
And that faint scar on his temple
Means nothing.

The light behind me is as clean
As the future:
Whatever past I've had is splintered
Like a looking glass.

I'm like a baby just born:
No worries, no shame or regret,
No guilt about the things I've done.
The women I've loved have let me start again.
I won't miss them or wet my pillow
With bitter tears.

Yesterday I searched my body inch by inch:
No tattoos or birthmarks, it meant nothing,
Like the body of any fifty year old man.
My lungs tell me I've never smoked
And my heart is steady as a clock.

I stare at my hands, try to recall
What they have touched, mended, broken.
My signature may have sealed contracts,
Warrants, treaties between nations:
I take a pen, fill a blank sheet with names,
Accuse myself of them, one by one.

I have this vocabulary in place,
This way of speaking
Which comes from nowhere.
They tell me that friends and family
Will be looking for me:
It is only a matter of time.

Whatever is lost may be found.
But when I saw that man in the dock
Trying to hand back his name –
Flashbacks to mass graves, flickering
White faces behind barbed wire – and
Witnesses accusing him across forty years,
I folded the sheet, found a clean envelope,
Posted it with no address.

A Mercenary Soldier
Turns for Home

I remember a blue line of hills
Glimpsed through sweat – always
A day's march away – hauling the guns
Towards their mirage, kites circling,
Grass whispering against our knees.

At night our fires died under stars
Scattered by frost, the yelps of dogs.
I stood sentry, braced against cold,
Counting winters camped under freezing easterlies,
A narrow-eyed people for neighbours.

In spring we burned their villages,
Took their cloth for our women, sabred
Theirs as they ran into the fields
From our lust: no other woman after
Ever yielded the wild taste of their fear.

Then, the years quickening, weariness,
Each campaign sickening like plague
In our veins, wanting each thaw, each truce
To wash us home with the wind at our backs,
Our youth quenched now like a thirst.

We came back, one by one, meeting
The blue lake of emptiness in the others' eyes,
Knowing what they had looked at.
The old men we would become had the same stare,
Gazing out to horizons brimming with cloud.

Rich men, we took wives, bred sons,
Taught them war games in the dust
Of the threshing floor; we told stories
Haltingly, our hands flailing meaning
From the gaps between words.

Each spring I watch for my boys to come:
Ice-floes break and float downstream,
Wind stirs grass, an ash of memories.
No speeches return, but the face of one woman
From a forgotten war, white and still amongst the corn.

Snow From The North

Tonight, snow comes squalling from the north:
It curfews streets to silence,
Smothers footsteps, car tyres, voices
From the golden doorways of pubs.

Driving into flickering ice-flames,
Rooftops are preened with cold's plumage;
Headlights glance on white wings
That beat in steady sweeps of snow.

The road dips and turns, brakes slew the car
Into invisible bends, tyres lurch
As it climbs in an agonising gear
Onto a hilltop where drifts bury the moor.

Below, lines of yellow lights waft out,
Wind spins its flakes over Burnley;
The town falls asleep, house by house,
Surrendering to the white bird's dreams.

Dead trees lean out from the dark:
Headlights amaze their eyeless staring,
Their lost souls clamour in the wiper blades,
Hiss under the tyres' treachery.

Only my hands between this and me:
They poke out from the grey cuffs of my coat,
Wrenching the car away where it swerves
Towards oblivion.

I'm home, those wings still kissing my face:
Up behind that window she's sleeping, not knowing
I'm here at last – still breathing, still holding
My breath – as snow lets that first star through.

Drowning at Pouzauges

The tip of his rod touched water,
Kissing it into quick dimples of light;
Sun baked the clay roofs of the town
Where it dozed on the hill,
Under the ruined chateau,
Under thudding afternoon heat
That drove the dull blood in his head.

There were damsel flies haunting
The water, dogs sniffing at his heels,
No clouds, and the cries of swimmers
On the lake's far edge chasing
Invisible fish his way.

His finger nails were puttied white
With another morning's dough –
Baguettes, ficelles, croissants –
His hands formed them, easy as sleep
Moulded dreams of the green lake's
Carp exhaling pure water.

He moved a few yards down the bank,
Flicking a float and baited hook
Onto his own shadow that swayed and wobbled
And eddied sideways as the waters shifted.
Tonight a full moon would cast itself
Upon this pale face: he would rise early
To see it wane in the valley's mist
As if it never had been real.

He felt the pull of it, the desire of it
Drawing him from his sleeping wife,
From the laundered sheets of their bed
To his work at the oven behind their shop.

Poplars and vineyards were sketched green
By an unsteady, heat-stricken hand;
The horizon's melting with sky was white-hot,
Hazing hour after hour into this late noon.
No sweat would cool his parched skin or soothe
The burns branding his wrists and arms.

His eye sank into a green iris of water,
He heard a rat plop into the reeds,
The hearts of fish pulsing,
Pumping their cold blood;
He heard the water sighing far-off words,
Meaningless as days that followed days.

No one saw his fall, but saw water-rings
Where a fisherman had been:
He did not rise to gulp a snatch of air
Or squander last breath in cries for help.
No past life flashed before his eyes
But a peace like emeralds, discovering
The lakes' lost treasure of sleep.

Photographic Memory

The footpath trails on beyond her
Into the brightest day;
Just a grey trace of cloud,
Stray leaves on the grass, though
It is early for them to fall.
The dog is blurred, like a genie
Metamorphosing into solid air.
She stands: a hand on the fence,
A hand on the walking stick,
Her cheeks bitten by wind,
Rinds of mud peeling from her shoes.

I remember the holiday, not this place:
All week the sea was high and grey,
Gulping our footprints from the beach.
A tea-room somewhere?
Apple or pear trees behind,
The cups thin and white as bone.
A check table-cloth, cores, crumbs.
The light is good, the shadows strong:
Her feet are clutched by them,
They eclipse her eyes like burnt moons
And she is smiling.

This light is too bright, coming
From the wrong direction.
Propped up in bed, it takes away her face,
Melts it into the white day outside net curtains.
Wisps of hair, everything misty,
An open book across her legs,
The clock stopped at 2.15, though
It ticked on over the hours and years.
A sixtieth of a second, f2.8 – no depth –
And blurred, the whole thing blurred,
As if my hand shook.

Night Ride: BMW R/80.

The road flicks away into the dark,
Bend after bend coming at him,
The headlight of the bike bobbing
On stone walls sheer as cliffs.

Young rabbits struggle to the verge,
Its glare tarring their feet to the road,
Dazing their fear, the engine's rage
Overwhelming their thin hearts.

The white house had shaken in his mirrors,
Its pale cloud drifting away. She had stood
By the window, drenched in his anger,
Watching his tailight dissolve into the dark.

Pistons hurtle in their scalding oil,
Horizontally opposed, but the camshaft turns
And the wheels turn, and the stars are at work
Like jewels in a slowing clock.

Wind tugs at his scarf,
Blurs everything with tears:
The speedo, the rev counter,
White lines suturing the road.

His lungs struggle against wild
Buffets of air,
His heart's valves tick
Into the last seconds of his will.

A Year of Dust

That's how they remembered it –
A blazing summer, a new house,
Dust getting everywhere:
Window ledges, chair arms, plates left out,
Hair which had to be washed each night
And dried next to their hot skin.

They recalled other summers –
Saharan sand and ladybirds blown in,
Experts explaining biblical plagues,
The death of the first-born a mere act of God away.

Outside the greengrocers' her fingers
Left green prints on the courgettes,
As if touching such plenty was a crime,
Her evidence smudging their chalky skins.

It was like ash from distant fires, or
Powdered bone from the city crematorium:
Fine, white, insidious, sifting slowly
Down the hourglass of the days.
The first time, he had put out a finger
And tasted it, bitter as a cud of lies.

It was the summer of their wedding,
Cameras stilling them in their vows,
The uneasy taste of desire:
They could not surrender,
As if to worship with their touch
Would betray what they so tightly held.

Later it was it was the autumn of hunger,
The Horn of Africa withering, fifteen
Million people starving, their credit card
Choking the telephone line with goodwill.
Yet hard to imagine that mass of people
As human, individual and alive.

It was the winter of the Gulf War,
The military murdering speech with
Precision bombing,
Pin-point accuracy,
Collatoral damage,
Their ordnance 'delivered' like mail.
And the hushed bodies coming home by night,
Stashed under airport lights, imported
To quiet applause on the commodities market.

It was the year of dust:
Inexplicable,
Deadly,
Taking its impression of the nation.

They ignored it now:
It settled over them as they slept,
Smooth as talc when they woke,
Falling softly from their folded clothes
As they dressed.

Dust in their throats,
Smothering them,
In their eyes,
Blinding them with tears:
Dust in their hearts
That would not be shaken off.

Mother and Son

All those months, trying to get out:
A word in a shut mouth, clenched
Into silence.
Only her booming heart
And the swaying dark pushing
Against the bone lid of her womb.

Now she is trying to escape into old age:
I won't let her go – she'd fly like a sparrow
Through the bars of my ribs,
Stop to touch this cracked one,
Or not fly, or sing, caged in me –

Her face going back behind the caul,
Her white hair drifting like smoke.

Frost

Last night, a thin blade of moon,
Stars pricking the blackness
Of time between each other.
This morning, frost-crystallised grass,
A bronze swarf of leaves turning
And dropping from the trees,
A big sun splintering light,
Shattering a still world of glass.

One magpie flies over the bus stop
Where our three sons stand,
Stamping like small ponies,
Panting dragon-statues
Of twisting breath.
A car exhaust smokes like battle
Through which they smile
And call out to me,
Chinking towards them
From the Post Office,
My pockets full of change,
My hands warming the nickel moons.

This morning you went without a word:
I watched from the window,
Wanting this dumbness,
Wanting to call you back.
You drove off through falling
Yellow poplar leaves
Into cold air, sun, time,
Into the distance between us:
Frost on the roof of the car,
Frost on our tongues,
A dawning sun molten above trees.

M6 Services

Between cities, we stop for coffee and fuel,
Watching as they pass:
The travellers, hurrying, eyes lowered,
Dragging their children to cafés or to pee,
Coins in their pockets jingling like keys.

Above us, neon signs burn our eyes
With good things to buy.
Outside, the afternoon blusters
Into darkness and wind,
Rain's silver needles stitching
Tiny parallels of light.

Raindrops sweat at the window,
Slip in crooked streaks, melting
The outdoors in their molten lens.
Glass doors open; their mirrors sway
Through chaotic angles of incidence.
Cold draughts blow through reflections
Which show us staring at ourselves:
Moving on, killing time,
Waiting for something to happen
Which would always be something else.

A tall man walks into the light,
Picking up the 'phone to tell his wife
That he is somewhere else.

Not here, where it is still raining
And there are trees with ruined nests
Standing against the sky.
Not here, where wind is moving litter,
As his tongue moves the lies in his mouth.

Somewhere else, that is not here,
Not here.

Unemployed at Tranmere: 1991.

Their white hands flutter,
Curling cigarette smoke
That quiet speech punches away;
Their knuckle-points maroon softly
Clenched fists beating to 'sixties singles
Spun from the juke-box.

Beyond this bar the shipyard clangs,
Tolling a far away busyness
Of labour and sweat and pay-days
Evaporating, vessel by vessel.
The river steals past, shifting
Its poisoned cargoes to the sea.

These men are waiting for a new scheme,
A new order, another half-pint:
Trades have fallen from their hands
Like money they could not save
Fell from their pockets,
Like days fall from the calendar,
Or ash from a trembling cigarette.

A door opens and swings shut,
Shocking the blue air with cold.
The men look up, greet him, look down;
All the old scores are forgotten
Or have died.

Through half-frosted windows
Telegraph lines are scrawled across
Sky's blank order-sheet, delaying
Pigeons who bear no other message
But their shit.

Another war would do the trick:
That incandescent vision of plenty,
Its ribbons of steel rolling from the forge
To plate another frigate.
But the new wars are far away,
And the dying is foreign and far away
Like an unaffordable holiday.

On the television, squaddies lug water
From landrovers to the blinding sand.
A helicopter lets out a general
Who holds his hat and salutes the dunes.
At New Brighton a trash of plastic
Lolls at the tide's edge.

In the corner the men glance up:
Someone swears, the barman laughs,
The dominoes go over, one by one.

Miss Devlin at the Sea View Hotel

A vase of blue iris on the sill,
Window glass streaked with dust,
The tide out, a far sea swelling
In slow glitters of light.

Wind tugs at marram on the dunes.
Fine insinuations of sand drift
Across the empty, still streets
Of the town.

Early and hopeful
A last fishing boat trawls,
Disappearing into smudged sea and sky:
Frontier between falling and drowning.

Above the bay herring gulls bank
Into quick slants of air,
A cormorant flies low and black
Over waves, purposeful as she is not.

***

Years before, walking on the beach,
She found a horse swallowed in sand,
Stood at the edge of a quaking crust,
Watching its brown flanks sweat
And sink, and sink.

Terrible the dumb head
Tilted to her,
Terrible the white eyes rolling
Towards an owner who had run for help
But run away.

Afraid of quicksand
She had reached out, but
Could not touch the muzzle.
She spoke and its ears flicked,
Accepting words like flies.

She remembered, days before,
Watching the same horse canter
Through sea-spray, fetlocks arching
Into waves that fell again and again
To stain white sand.

She stayed, saw its nostrils flare,
Its teeth bite at air and life,
Until she could not look, turned away
From the men with ropes and boards, from
The weeping girl who reached for the reins.

In the newspaper that night
She found the horse's useless name:
How they had fought to drag it back,
Had reclaimed it, dead,
All 'heroic' efforts vain.

***

Men from the Magnox plant up-coast
Unpack geiger counters from their van,
Pacing the beach like feeding waders,
Step by step.

Each day she watches them,
Feeling salt dry on her skin,
Feeling the sea stilled in her arms
Like a child lulled to sleep.

In a few more years...
The thought dries up slowly like a tear.
She pushes a button, watches the screen
Light up with today's news.

Mobs crowd streets in a hot country,
A man lies crumpled at the check-point,
Houses burn, a line of refugees
Walks towards her through the night.

A baker's van tilts round the corner:
Gulls, balancing on chimney pots,
Gorged with the sea's gifts,
Wake the town with their cries.

Passing Out

A line of swallows on the wire outside,
Between them on the table breakfast plates,
A blue telegram meagre with words
As with regrets.

They tried to picture the place
Where he had died:
A hot country with sand and flies,
Undrinkable water, beggar children:
Sores on their legs, mosquitos
Drinking from the corners of their eyes.

She pushed back a strand of hair,
Wondering if he had thought of them.
He watched the clock from habit,
Watched the door.
The company would dock his pay,
His lathe stilled, coils of bronze
Spilling to the workshop floor.

She could not speak, but put the kettle on;
Water's tattoo rolled brittle as a drum.
They saw the swallows shift and rise, pulled
Airwards by their invisible urgency
To be gone.

The telephone rang, a reporter
From the newspaper had heard:
Could they confirm? Could she call
To do a story on their son?

Stalled in the spotlight of his death
They agreed.
She fetched the family album
And they sifted through, seeing
Him grow taller on each page:

From Chaplin in the school charade
To squaddie at his passing out parade.
And they were lost again in pride
That killed their rage.

Mole Totem

They jerk on the wire,
Death's agony bitten
Between heavy-duty jaws.

Their paws still swim through
Earth-dark, bone flippers
Poised for each stroke.

Backs convulse against wind,
Rain washes strychnine
Through their leaky spines.

They snapped like high wires:
The lives that tip-toed fell
Into the seasons' oblivion.

Moleskin dries over ribs' white
Basketwork, the brown husks sway:
Airborne seeds of a subterranean will.

One by one they fall, softened
By April rain – quicken – plunge
Blindly back into waves of soil.

Home in April

Home is empty:
Guitars are asleep in black cases,
The ashen fires smell of soot.

Silverfish shiver in the hearths,
Letters pile up against the door
Like snow.

Children's voices have blown away
Into the broken poplar tree;
Their footsteps pour down the empty street.

The telephone rings,
Its voices penned like damned souls
Behind the shrill bell.

Under acheing rafters eight generations
Of the dead rub shoulders.
Woodworm rock in their oak hammocks.

Window glass thins against Yorkshire air,
The moon's face presses in upon
A house sighing with empty beds.

Hills are tarnished with silver cloud;
The farmer, his coat tied with string, drives
Up the lane towards lambs dazed with life.

Climbing With a Dead Man

The day he fell his cry grabbed at sky,
His body's dark star wheeled the void:
I held him, belayed, took the strain,
Until he climbed back past me spewing blood.

At every hold his eyes dulled with hate,
At every rest he coiled the rope's long
Hiss, betrayed to rock that bears us, that
Licks us with a black, parched tongue.

This morning we woke on the totem of the crag:
It reared dumbly, fractured, bare.
Later, sun will pinion moves across its sleep,
Our fingers sweating on its dreams of air.

He makes the moves and I follow, nudged
By thermals, testing each flake.
Questions piton deep into my stone-numb,
Fissured mind: it is days since he spoke.

I climb his chimneys slippery with blood,
Lodge my feet on red stains leaked from his toes:
He takes the rope but does not see,
His eyes torn out by screaming hawks.

The night of the day he fell, I dreamed
Of rain lashing rock, blue ropes ablaze
With lightning, St. Elmo's fire
Spidering between us on the drenched face.

But his shoulders were heaving towards
Some hold in that hurricane of night,
Hands bearing down to raise his body to a ledge,
Balanced on a flickering crux of light.

Now a raven comes close to watch us,
Its wing-tips scattering clouds' white spores:
It rides their solidity like waves,
Its eye sees life leaking from our pores.

I have forgotten how many days we have climbed,
His empty eyes are blind to time:
I say that we are hands on a clock-face of rock,
His purple tongue lolls and I bite mine.

He takes the rope, I gasp for it,
Face grazed against the shark-skin rock,
Sun falls back behind its splintered spines:
Each night he chooses the ledge to bivouac.

No sleep: canvas flaps with moans of the dead
Who cling to this stone needle without hope.
At dawn I ask him if he has heard their cries,
He shakes his eyeless head and coils the rope.

He makes the moves and I follow,
He gives me rope, I take it, tasting fear.
The rock twins us, hold by hold:
I see myself, the void, steps reaching into endless air.

Above Grasmere

'The Kurds have no friends.'
                    Proverb

Slow ripples puckered the lake,
Its sheet steel crumpling shorewards;
Thorns caught her legs as she climbed
Above waterborne pulses of light.
A cold wind numbed her face,
Slipstreamed her in its dragnet of air.

At the summit she turned to face hills
Running green in outbursts of sun.
A mob of gulls greeted her,
Black-headed, young, insistent,
Confusing the sky with their wings
And cries.

Impatient, gone on ahead,
He was waiting for her,
Cradled in the rock.
The smell of his cigarette
Turned her from the perfect view
Where a silver van
Went up the road like mercury
Towards good weather.

Beyond the distance in her eyes
Other mountains rose up:
A nation bivouaced in mud,
Scrambling at the screen's edge,
Tins of baby milk tumbling
Into turbulent, freezing air.

Each day on the news:
Cultivating the stones
On their children's graves,
Their English halting,
Their clothing quaint as a nativity.

They were there and she was here, breathless,
Climbing above the town, last patches
Of snow picturesque against the fells.

He rose smiling from his shelter,
A grass stalk in his teeth,
The cigarette stubbed,
His hands reaching into her jacket,
Warm as bread for which the gulls rose
And stooped and cried.

Storm in Suburbia

Blackshaw Head

On impulse, she took the helmet
And they rode off on his bike,
Not caring what others thought who
Flawed their snatched moments.

She sat behind, wearing
His leather jacket:
He shivered in shirtsleeves
At the throttle, powering
The machine up through a
Dizzy gravity of bends
That strove to drag them back
Into Calderdale.

They took the road to Blackshaw Head,
Following stone walls, awed by
A blood-stained October moon,
Its fluid sac leaking light
Onto the black outline of hills.

All the way he felt her pressed
To his spine, her legs just touching
His as they swayed into bends,
Tilted down blind slopes.
All the houses were closed up,
Lit or sleeping.
A car passed, branking them
With a white mask of light.

Grasses turned over under wind,
Sheep's eyes glanced from the moor.
He reached the crossroads,
Cut the engine, held the bike upright
As she stumbled off, burning
Her leg on its hot silencer.
Ignoring the pain, she inhaled
His scent zipped into leather
That creaked around her.

He took her hand:
They walked to the hill's ridge,
Looking out to where townships cast
Up a yellow haze and farm lights
Stuttered against articulate blackness.

Clouds tore the moon's membrane,
Barring their faces with shadow;
Lapwings still trickled their calls
Into shuddering air masses
That shifted westward.

He held her, hands inside his
Own jacket, the thin skirt
Rumpling, her fingers cool on his neck.
They bent their heads, each tasting
Thirst in the other's mouth:
He shivered, abandoned
To a momentum of falling air,
His tongue defining her dumbness.

The purple scar burned on her leg
And still she said nothing:
Beside them the bike gleamed,
Tilted on its stand at the angle
Of the Earth's turning.

Visiting Time

She waited for him,
Pillowed up in bed,
Willows shivering under
A uniform grey sky,
Rain drenching the last light.
She was hungry,
Lost in the swish of tyres,
Lost in their footsteps,
Walking away.

A nurse came to tuck her in:
Cool hands, cool skin
Touching hers.
The thermometer clicked
Against her teeth,
Her fever pushing its silver
Higher and higher.

She saw the poplars' bare wires,
Almost touching,
The fall of their leaves
Yellowing the grass,
She heard the tick of an engine,
Saw raindrops tremble
On the window's blurred caul.

And then his hand
Holding hers, his tongue
Stammering through a litany
Of delays.
She hugged her belly
Between the silences,
Felt the child fighting
Her body
And winning.

And all the time
Their heels clicking,
Their voices,
Walking away.

Storm In Suburbia

Black cloud moving eastward,
Swallowing last light from leaves
That are too green on the birch tree
Outside her window.

Her breasts ache with new milk:
She touches them as her child
Sleeps in its basket. Outside,
Traffic slows as the lights change.

Thunder cracks above the town hall steeple,
Blue tangs of electricity
Rip open a sky
Pregnant with cumulus.

The woman watches her hands
As they rock the basket.
She thinks of Soweto women
Drawing water in tins,

Their mothers hands, black as roots,
Wave flies from sleeping children:
She thinks of Warsaw, tanks quartering the ghetto,
Yellow stars pinned under dead faces.

She sees a pillar of cloud
Swallowing the lost tribes;
Her breasts ache with milk
For a child born into the atom's rage.

Traffic moves on under green lights,
Thunder grumbles, drops of rain
Rattle on the window like grain.
Leaves shudder and gleam.

She sees gutters running with water:
Sheet lightning, rain-needles, clouds
Black as bible covers, and the child,
Waking, wailing, reaching out to her.

Skimming

She sat on the plaid rug.
He stood with their daughters
At the very edge of the lake,
His hand whipping flat stones
Out across a glaze of breaking light.
It hurt her eyes to see them skip
And explode in sun, two small girls
Laughing at his heels, clapping hands
As the skimmers launched, turned
At the limit of their range,
Then reared and sank.

Behind her larch trees simmered
In a faint breeze, a goldcrest
Flickered from the branches, plumage
Dazzling their smouldering green.
She caught the scent of larch as she screwed
The cap from the thermos and called to him.

He ran hand in hand with the girls
Back from the lake:
They tumbled at her feet
Shouting questions, their hands
Spilling sand into the picnic.
She shushed them, wiped them clean
And they ate.

The first clouds, tipped grey
Like pigeon feathers, plumed
Up from hills beyond the lake.
Coniston went leaden as they watched,
The chill raised goose-flesh
On their bare arms;
They put on cardigans, let the girls
Run back to the shallows to play.

A ring-dove called from the wood,
Throaty with desire;
She felt his hand on her calf,
Stroking her skin as they drank
And their children broke the blank water
With stones.

His touch was gritty with sand:
Tiredness pulled her down to the rug,
And he was smiling, young, sunburned
As in the photographs they took home,
Holding out his cup to ask for more.

Revolution

As she waited a cigarette curled smoke
Into her hair;
The children asleep in bed, his meal
Cooking in the oven, both their places set.

At six the telephone rang and his voice
Answered hers: some trouble with the car,
The battery dead, a colleague to run him home,
He'd be an hour, with things to finish off.

She cleared a space, spread open her books
At the French Revolution and read.
Robespierre, Marat, Diderot, the Supreme Being:
Their names tumbrilled through her head.

She checked the children, their pillows damp
With dreams, stooping to hear a car whisper
Under the birch tree, watching from upstairs
As their heads touched briefly.

Then his key was panting in the lock:
Kissing her, he was sorry to be late,
A mechanic would come tomorrow, mend the damage -
She set down their meal and they ate.

Silences rustled in the skirting board,
Flapped curtains from an open window;
She saw how his eye dreamed towards tomorrow,
How his lips guillotined her question.

Saturday Class

Shadows of her hand crossed the paper
As the classroom emptied:
Dust glinted in a solid bar of sun,
Footsteps shuffling in the corridor,
Voices emptying through green doors
As she set down the last word.

Outside, clutching a Kit-Kat,
Wind ruffled her hair,
She thought of the journey home
Stretching to the unmade bed,
To dishes greasing the sink,
His socks still on the floor,
His last accusation bruising the air.

A corporation rubbish truck convulsed,
Venting grey diesel fumes;
A couple, younger then them,
Threw in a mattress.
The slots of a grid gaped,
Wind touched her face,
Dark trees bulked on the hillside.

He would be gone already:
His creel packed,
His sandwiches made,
The rod-bag over his shoulder,
Their children at his mother's.
She leaned against the wall,
Catching the dusty scent of brick:
In her mouth chocolate was as sweet
As lies she could not tell.

A starling's shadow jinked over,
Sun shrank behind a cloud.
Shivering, she went in,
The classroom still empty,
The door handle cold in her fingers.
She saw his face above still water,
His eyes reflected, dark as embers.

Here, a row of cups,
The faint scent of coffee,
Sun burnishing air's dust.
She ran her fingers over a stained rim,
Heard the first faint footsteps
Treading silence towards her.

The Call

She'd decided the night before,
Browsing over her books in the kitchen,
Writing notes, watching
As he skinned the rabbit
Bought cheap from a market stall:
His fingers pulled out its heart
Like an oracle.

The childred, horrified, had wept:
He worked patiently, tugging
At the pelt, reminding them
Of redder meat they'd eaten
Without shame:
They went guility upstairs,
Guarding their teddy bears.

In bed his hands had smelt
Of blood.
She'd shrugged him off, wrapping
Herself around her closed thighs.

His mouth tried to say it:
How he loved, hated, pitied her,
How he wanted her and always would,
How this silence left him falling
From her into emptiness.
Vainly, trying to fly that distance,
His words circled like moths
Drawn to her mute, corrosive flame.

That morning she'd dialled
The number in her head
And a friend's voice
Had simply answered 'Yes'.
She packed her bags
And one for the girls –
Nothing unnecessary –
From school she'd drive them far away.

He'd come home to her curt note:
An ashtray piled with stubs,
A stack of skewerd bills,
The rabbit, curled like a foetus
In the fridge.

Mushrooming

He searched for their ingot whiteness
Through dusk, stumbling down the bank,
Under the black branches of an ash.
Crouching, he felt for them,
Groping, pulling on their stems
Until they broke free from roots,
Their hymens snapping under his hand.

Headlights from the road below
Pressed his shadow onto ridges
Of downward flowing earth;
Sheep coughed a mist of breath,
The smell of soil reached for him.
Deceived by lambs' tails, wool, dung,
His fingers were blind, feeling
In damp grass for their pale corruption.

The bag grew heavy in his hand:
Light failed him, kneeling
In a smoke of darkness to pull
The last few mushrooms from earth.
A single woodcock planed overhead:
He rose, turned for home, slithered in clay.

The crash of cars on the road below
Echoed from the banking:
He heard a far-off shouting,
Saw slewed lights, then people
Silhouetted, black and frantic as ants.

He stood, imagining granules
Of the windscreen sticky with blood,
A woman cradling a man's head in her lap,
Her mouth opening to swallow the night
In one dumb scream, then the silence,
On the outside of everybody, touching him too.

Heels clicking against stones,
He walked down to the gate, through
The garden, past lines of washing
Into the light of his own kitchen
Where the skillet, the pepper pot,
The bottle of beer lay ready.

He stood at the sink, weighing
His hoard, washing its black
Newsprint of spores from his fingers.

Mending his Motorcycle in Wartime

He was in their bomb sights
And he knew it, kneeling
With his hands inside the engine's
Cold mechanics, splitting his nails
On its seized-up parts.
They perfected their delivery
And in their very flight path
He crouched before his dead god.

All morning they scorched the air
Above the village,
And all morning he tested relays,
Replaced burned wires, coaxed the engine,
Caressed it, pleaded with it to live.

It was no use.
The planes panicked him,
Closing up his ears like deep water.
He worked too fast,
His hands blackened with oil,
The faults evading him;
Their little untruths snagged together
Into one impossibility.

He walked back to the house for coffee,
Noticed snowdrops drooping their heads,
Crocuses wide open, purple as sudden flames
In February sun.

Still the bombers came, shaking rooftiles,
Making the kitchen windows hum;
He washed his hands and still they came,
Lower and lower,
Practising their runs over his house,
His garden, his abandoned machine.

The news was all bad, though
They they said it was good:
Allied casualties were light,
The ground-attack was racing on.
But across those hopeful foreign maps
The dead were dead, their futures
Stopped like dud cheques,
Their credit cancelled, and dollars
Falling from bomb-bays by the ton.

They were dying horribly, but the day
Went on just as surely towards night,
The light ebbing, closing up the flowers,
Imperceptible as their breathing.

He walked back to the bike,
Carrying a steaming mug,
Scalding his throat
With the anguish if it all.
A jet rolled away slowly, towing
Its scream, nippled with warheads,
Camouflaged the colour of sand over green fields
Where first lambs stumbled to life.

At last, unsuspected,
He found the broken wires,
Cleaned them, touched them together
In a scatter of blue sparks:
The engine fired, joyfully turned
Then stalled, lying still as his hands
Moved apart to let silence fall.

Family Reunion

Going back, he drowned,
Fell from her hands like a child
And sank.
She could do nothing
But gaze at her palms,
Watch him drift in white water.

He fell and she saw
Him spiral slowly back,
His face blubbery,
His cries lungless, swallowed
By the black cave
Of his father's mouth.

Nearly forty now and sleepless,
But at three in the morning
The face at the window
In the echoing street
Still watched for him.

In bed, lights of cars
Closed over him like
The hum of the mill,
His mother's breathing
In the next room,
A neighbour's baby wailing
Through the walls.

When he rose it was to magpies
Squabbling in the garden,
Engines waking on the lorry park,
New houses filling
The valley's thin scoop:
A sycamore tree erect
In its coffin of earth,
Still dying,
Still trying
To heal his name.
He stroked her face
Where she lay dozing.

Later their sons leaned
Over the canal bridge,
Fishing for shadows
In softly flowing water:
He told them of giant pike,
Perch that slashed hands
With their spines,
Tench with terrifying
Rubber lips,
Of a line of policemen, thirty
Summers ago, beating
White mist from willow herb
Towards a drowned boy.

She heard and was afraid:
He'd gone under too deep
And she could not swim,
Had not expected this -
That a man could breathe water
And still live in her life.
She saw his face, his father's face
Drifting closer and closer,
Their children pointing,
Excited, dipping the surface
With questions.

At the brook's black water
They asked him if fish
Had ever swum that liquid stink:
He told them no, staring,
Not telling how this stream
Had been the well-spring
Of his world, how in sleep
Time ebbed from his eyes
And he still dreamed
And woke dreaming
Of water, like wine
Clearing over emerald weed,
Its fish gravid, baptised by light,
The current giving up its dead.

Kill

*'And men will not understand us...the years will
pass by and in the end we shall fall into ruin.'*

Erich Maria Remarque

He walked back to the village:
The mountains were green,
As still as if reflected in deep water,
But shining on the backs of his eyes
They moved dizzily against sky.

He climbed higher to a plateau of fields,
The houses of his people.
Below, the forest steamed in hot mist.
He squinted, expecting each second
To bring rockets, helicopters, a machine-gun's
Iron heart beating at the hatchway.

Rain speckled dust on the track,
His feet scattered hens,
An old woman shaded her eyes
And watched him come closer.
His tongue was dry and heavy,
It moved the word in his mouth
Like a stone.

A mongrel inched sideways towards him:
That was his father in the doorway,
His mother in the fields, younger,
Still supple as she stooped and rose
In a drifting smoke of rain.

They would want him to take a woman,
To work the land,
To set aside what he had been
Or was.

Here were hills they had never climbed:
He had bivouacked on other peaks,
Told stories of this place,
Watching for lights,
Seeing tracer rounds spark and fall
Like planets into darkness.

The dog knew him, its high yelp
Jerked up his mother's face,
Disbelieving and too far away.
His father's hand was on his arm:
Almost blind, he peered towards
The memory of a lost son.

And the word was stuttering
At his lips,
Falling into him,
Making him dumb, falling into him
As his mother lifted up her skirts
And ran weeping, laughing, weeping
Towards him through the rain.

Guy Fawkes' Night

That year they were driving home as fires
Lit up dark wastelands all across the town:
Oily smoke, sparks dying in the road,
Their children's faces flat to the car windows.

Rockets arced upwards, shrieking,
Showering orange stars above the streetlamps.
Demolition timbers crackled, guys burned,
Words slithered in their parched mouths.

He wanted to tell her what she already knew,
Or guessed, or had been told by a wagging tongue:
There was someone else. Someone else who had touched,
Held, tasted him. Their lips were dry as touch-paper.

He braked at the traffic lights and revellers
Crowded the windows, wordlessly laughing;
The children fell into silence, staring
As fires boiled paint from all the house-fronts.

Her face was white under scatters of light;
She pulled her skirt down over her knees,
Played with the hem of her jacket, watched him.
Outside, their faces were lit masks, jeering.

At last it was their own driveway, their own still house,
And on their lawn the children's surprise:
A pyre of sticks, an effigy pointing skywards,
The blaze already imagined in their father's head.

The Fall

He bled from a quartz womb
Onto the rock,
Staining it with his birth
And it mothered him:
Centuries clinging
Like an egg,
An embryo
Wrapped in spiders' webs,
Shrouded, coming into the future,
Signalling himself like weather,
Holding his breath
Like a prophecy.

The rock was blasted out
Block by block,
Hewn by navvy-gangs,
Carted to build a city.
Bewildered, as the stones
Lurched into place,
As the foundations set,
He began to climb,
Forcing his bones into rock.

Above neon advertisements,
The sodium canyons of streets,
He climbed towards sky,
Upwards,
Jamming his fists
Into ancient crevices of stone.

It mothered him
With drifts of cloud,
With secretions of fern,
Acres of glass,
Lungs of carbon monoxide,
With lead-coated alveoli,
It mothered him
With the countless deaths
Of the night.

He was a man
And the rock was his mother:
His puzzlement forced him higher,
He licked the rock like a breast,
Guzzling its black milk.

In summer, sun hammered him
Into its grooves:
A peg of bone,
A girder of muscle
Spanning himself above the void.

In winter he climbed white
Beards of ice,
Burning his lips on their
Slowly dripping water.

He slept with his fists
Locked into stone,
Dreamed of a city
Spiralling in dust,
Of a hot wind levelling
The skyline,
Of a huge sun fusing the crystals
Under his hands.
He woke to grey light
Smearing his eyes,
His muscles groaning awake,
His tendons snapping against bones'

Tormenting tension.

Each day he left a new layer
Of skin on the rock,
Shedding himself cell by cell:
Office workers watched from windows,
Shoppers in the street looked up.
His corpuscles dried
In the stone pores of rock,
His semen boiled in the sun
Like pearls.

The rock was his mother
And his father was a rock,
A war memorial,
An erect pillar engraved
With remembrance
Under a pregnant moon.

He climbed on,
Tortured by his memory of sky.
He clung
Above the traffic roundabouts,
Above the subways,
Above the shopping centres,
The town hall, the courts of law.
And the city held its breath
As he rose on the body of his mother
Into the seduction of wind
That stroked his thighs
And begged him to fall.
He stuffed his ears
With the dung of birds, climbed
Above the telephone wires
With their simmering messages,
Above the pylons
With their blue voltages,
Wearing their glass insulators
As a necklace, a charm

Against the visions
That shocked through his sleep.

He perched on ledges with pigeons,
Called with the voice of starlings
Into streets where whores stood
Like jays outside fast food cafes
And pimps watched traffic
Pause before their golden girls.
He hung his shadow above the city,
Above the abyss of night:
Through darkness he saw
Children running for home,
Vagrants asleep in doorways,
Drunks stumbling blind and lonely
From empty bars:
Their nightmares rose up around him like a pall.

The smoke of the city crematorium
Made his flesh immortal.
Its fumes darkening his skin,
Tanning it to a pelt,
Polluting his teardrops,
Embalming him like a pharoah;
And all the time he heard water
Gushing through the stone,
Bleeding from the source
Of the rock,
Its dammed voices calling him.

In the hospital the sick
Fell comatose under white sheets
Of ether, one by one:
The climber mantled through their sleep,
Through the black headlines,
The pointed telephoto lenses,
The TV cameras
And the newsreels,
Until they forgot

That he still climbed, hung, dreamed,
Thinking that he must have fallen,
That he had reached some summit,
The gourd of his head withering
Among the stars.

But he climbed on until
Bones grew through his hands,
Unfurling like ferns.
His toes' stumps scrabbled
Against cornices, ledges, balconies,
Against the crumbling gutterwork.
He climbed on, gangrenous with age
Over the sculpted arêtes.
His eyes became the white eyes
Of a sick bird,
A slow mebrane focussing the architecture
Under his grip.
He dreamed of gulls flocking
On the city dump,
Their blizzard of wings,
Their hunger pulling at him
Where he weakened like a scab
Bled from the rock.

And when he fell his mother
Shrugged him off like rain.
When he fell his father
Offered his flank for a name,
Shouldering into the sun
On another, new day.
And the climber hung
In the shreds of time,
In the shrouds of the city's future
In the shadow of the fire-storms,
Alone.

On Caton Road

The road's black skin glistened,
Sloughing dawn's glimmer of light;
The motorcycle coughed, shuddered,
Panted white smoke, poisoned a morning
Frosted in drifts of powdered glass.

Dark silver clouds blew over,
Mist hushing the river to the sea.
Cold air that blasted you,
Seconds ahead,
Stung my eyes with ice, paralised
These hands where they steered the bike,
Numbed my clenched mouth with speed.

Then, suddenly, your blue Suzuki
Crumpled in the road,
Half-darkness, a line of cars
Blinking down the diversion,
People running for help.
But you lying alone –
As if you'd sinned – broken,
With your unbatheable wound,
One hand held out, an oilstain
Bleeding around you.

I knelt on frozen tarmac, feeling
For a pulse, pulling up an eyelid
To see your pupil narrow at the light:
It stared back, wide, empty, black.

A woman's coat laid over you
Where you lay across white lines.
Headlamps, veiled by fumes,
Wept light over us:
Mine still burning,
Yours smashed in the road,

My breath blossoming to steam,
Yours, a crushed flower petalled
In your chest, unfurled fingers
Curling slowly, the car that killed you
Clucking as it cooled.

I loosened your helmet, pulled
The scarf from your dumb mouth;
Your blood smearing my hands,
Your thin wrist signalling nothing,
As if my premonition cheated you of life,
Kneeling amongst crazed lights,
Your knuckles' white dice spilled from my hand.

When the ambulance came they lifted you in:
A fatality whose wallet would hold all the clues.
I turned for home, steered
Towards the locked house of tomorrow
For which there is no key.

Dawn melted through blazing clouds,
Throwing my shadow on the verge:
Carburretors breathing cold clear air,
Tailpipes hoarse with lust for the road,
The police already searching for your name.
And me, with your dead eyes in mine,
Speeding away through a brilliant morning.

Boy with Dead Mole

You were out in the park, playing
With fallen chestnut boughs
And we were bombing the Basra road,
Mopping up an army in the wreckage
Of their armour and their pride.

Outside, wind was tugging at sycamore trees
And there might be snow, isobars scowling
Across the weather man's electronic map.
It was a winter of maps, their low pressure
Drawing in the weather's steel.

You walked in, ten years old,
Cradling a dead mole in your hands,
Calling 'Daddy' into the room.
You held it for me, soft, blind,
Curled as a leaf blackens under frost.

It should have been sleeping,
Dreaming new labyrinths through soil,
Shoring up a fortress of dark;
But some change in the weather
Or trembling of the earth
Roused it to die in the open.

We were hunting down conscripts
In the desert;
Oil-wells were mourning sky
With black plumes of smoke;
An ocean's slicks were licking
At its drowned seabirds.

You were calling 'Daddy', holding out
A dead mole whose paws forced apart the day,
Darkness leaking through the crack.
You held it, wanting it to live:
I held you and wind took our house
And shook it.

An Irish Bishop in Peru

He watches soldiers goose-step in the square:
Huancavelica's public prosecutor, a pair
Of army colonels, close behind.
Each soldier's face a red-black rind
Of camouflage paint, though it's not yet night
And there is nothing to hide from but the light.

At his house a letter sealed from Rome:
It warns him to be 'circumspect', whilst one from home
Tells of cold Antrim rain and labour on the farms.
Soldiers boots crash, shouldering arms they
Climb into the truck; a British camera crew are there
To capture peasant faces blanked out by despair.

The journalists came to see him, played their tape.
It catalogues the Disappeared, death, torture, rape.
Angel Escobar Jurado's gone: his wife cries
Out for justice, hearing official lies
Nail down the certainty that he is dead:
No resurrections granted, but Te Deums of lead.

A man in hiding tells haltingly through tears
How they trussed, hung, martyred him for days.
This woman shows how soldiers bowed her head:
A communicant three point-blank bullets left for dead.
'Of course there have been excesses, they will pass,
Some of the soldiers come to celebrate my mass.'

Helicopters darken sky, a swarm ordained
To break these whispering huddles as they form.
The Bishop turns to go, knowing it's too late when
Droughts of faith are slaked by sacraments of hate.
Too late to dream of Ireland, write his learned tome,
Too late to break the silence spreading out from Rome.

Soldiers' eyes are stones behind their rifle stocks:
The tongues of priests have grown as still as rocks.

Invasion

He sat on the stairs
Pulling tacks from the old carpet,
Cursing the last owner,
Drinking Glenmorangie from a wine glass,
Outstaring a row of Barley White paint cans.

He'd got it all to do:
She was working late, the kids
Had fallen asleep over their books.
He'd pulled 'Great Escapes' from under
The eldest's curls and laughed.

He made some toast, watched the news:
Iraqi troops in Kuwait,
A US task force ready to sail,
Oil prices up, share prices fallen,
A minor war in Liberia, but real people
Lying dead on that track.

The weather-man brought a clearing sky:
A good night for star gazing.
He imagined the whole street
Staring up through sodium lights,
Doors thrown open to show immaculate
Hallways and stairs.

He remembered a bare attic, the set
Of shell lampshades made in Bali:
He went back to work, pulled out
A bent tack and broke his nail.
As the thumb went into his mouth
He saw her arms around their necks.

The boss, the accountant, the errand boy:
Any bastard could fill his space.
He went upstairs, smashed the shades,

Then watched Newsnight with a full glass,
Smiling as oil and blood ran out over sand,
Rising as a car door slammed outside.

Anfal

> Kurdish refugees, winter 1991.

Rain, smoking in across the mountains,
Chilled his ears and eyes:
Down there the rocks were swarming,
Their clothing crucified on thorns
To dry or tatter in the wind.

Still more than enough light
And the rock textured like iron:
Shutter-speed, aperture, exposure -
The camera felt cold as a gun.

He screwed forward the lens,
Stopped-up the light to blur
A background of burnt-out cars
And heaped Kalashnikovs,
Isolating a child whose mother
Lay sick under polythene sheets:
Their opaque prayer-flags flapped at sky,
Then froze on his negative.

More rain, hail, clouds brimming
With the horizons' escaping light;
They were shouting him from the van,
Wanting to move on, to see more.

He would rather work for an image here:
A helicopter dropping food against cascades
Of scree, that old woman's mouth,
Silhouetted, toothless, cursing heaven.

He watched it pass in fractions of seconds,
Each one divisible by light or dark.

Later, in the television studio,
Unshaven, his best prints flashed
Into five million homes,
They would ask him about the danger,
A worsening situation,
The scale of the tragedy.

And he would remember their faces,
Burned into the black rings under his eyes;
Would hear their voices shattering a mountain,
Falling into valleys impossibly far away.

Webs

The web is hardly there, visible only
When stray light discovers it.
Dew drops wobble – globed oil slicks
On taut silk – a cranefly blunders in,
Smashes droplets and sticks,
Its girder-work legs desperately pumping,
Glued to silk hawsers that pulled it from sky.

The boy writes in dust with his bare toe,
Behind him a train is slowing down.
Soldiers stare from its windows,
Their uniforms the only green where sand
Flows away into the bleached blue of their eyes.
The water butt has dried out,
Cuts sting on the boy's face,
A thin line of ants heads nowhere,
Carrying nothing.

Silk shudders and shudders
As the fly pulls its legs, trying
To make them work, zithering
The air with flicking wings;
The spider scuttles out onto invisible rigging.
Its eyes are full of victims,
The shroud unravels from its womb.

The boy watches a man's shadow
Walk towards him over the stones;
He has been told what to say
But the words are stuck in his gullet,
Trapped like birds, their dry plumage
Feathering his mouth with silence.

The web vibrates, the cranefly
Becomes a luminous blur;
The spider waits, patient, watching it tire,

Knowing the silk cage will not snap.
There is nothing here
That it has not seen before,
That it will not see time and time again.

The man smiles, his hand on the holster.
Sun touches clouds that will not bring rain,
Burns through onto plumes of dust
Scuffed up by his boots:
The train shunts forward –
An inch, an inch, an inch.

A Matchstick Model
of the Forth Bridge

He lay in the hollow of her body,
Nested in the warm smells of the bed;
Orange light petered through curtains
Hastily drawn the night before.

Another day: waiting for the giro,
The second Test against India,
Her grey face drifting about the house,
Seeing only what he was now.

He got up to make the tea; she groaned,
Shifting against him. He ran his hand
Down her spine. Thin as a whippet
And a tongue quicker off the mark.

In the kitchen he plugged in the kettle,
Found a bin liner spilling scraps, carried it
Out to the yard. Wakes week: seven more days
Until council men came for the black bags.

Sun was burning-in silhouettes of roofs,
Taunting the street to come awake.
On a day like this he'd have been first on the site,
Brewing up in the hut, a few sweet minutes alone.

Next to him the bags hummed, electrified
By trapped bluebottles. He thought of it,
Their whole lives spent in the dark, laid
And hatched on the refuse of his life.

Flies, maggots: the whole yards would be crawling
In this heat. He shuddered and went in.
The newscaster's voice brought a downward trend
In employment, a rise in the FT index.

He carried tea to the bedroom, shook
Her awake. She reached for her cigarettes,
Coughed, gave him the spent match for his tin.
He took it, shambled back downstairs.

She blew smoke into unbearable light,
Hearing him move about the house, seeing him
Lift the base-board, Stanley knife, glue,
The half-finished structure bridging his day.

When she came down to make breakfast
He would already be at work.

An Eel at Lake Coniston

The night sky blowing westwards,
A quarter moon silvering those star-
Swallowing shoals of cloud.

Scents of wet grass bruise underfoot,
Sheep bleat across meadows, whispers
Smoke from our frozen mouths.

The lake is glimpsed through willows,
Lights of the drowned town lapping
On its pewter gleam.

We find the jetty, walk out,
Lie down to smell the rot of timber
That sways beneath us as we breathe.

Our torches light up liquid glass
Dense with water mites; they
Flicker in a sudden electric dawn,
Swimming unafraid in its ecstasy.

Then I see it, turning above the gleam
Of snagged fishing line, a torque
Coiling and uncoiling, an eel, greenish,
Finned like a fish but flowing landwards.

From the Sargasso, too deep for nets
Or lights it has swum here to rise
At this instant, its eyes lamping
The reeds for prey.

A rumour,
A warning,
A premonition destined
At the water's broken rim.

You didn't see it, deny it, yet
Want it to slide into the light:
Our torch beams search this cold crucible
Where I know it moves under us.

Invisible under the town's reflection,
Choosing its element, shy of its own legend,
It moves, beautiful as we are now, beautiful
And fierce with hope under this torn sky.

THE RED FIELD

The Red Field

Leonard

I am in the red field;
Alone in the red field.

Hannah is asleep.
Her back is warm,
Turned from me like a soft wall:
My fingers run up the knobbles
On her spine.
Then it comes,
Up through my fingers,
Up through this patchwork
Stitched from blackness,
Frightening me,
Spinning me away until
I know I will be lost forever.

Then Hannah will begin to look for me
In all the corners of all the fields.

I am in the red field:
Hannah is crying,
Not asleep,
With those hands touching her
Over and over.
She does not see me,
Running like a matchstick man,
She does not see me
Pulling at the gate.
Tears wet her face,
Her body is thin in the white nightdress
That winds around her.

I'm calling out
But my mouth makes the wrong shape,
Says the wrong sounds.
I've been stitched into the quilt.
I want to shout out, over and over:
'I'm in the red field!
The red field!'

But her face turns slowly away
Leaving the moon there,
Cold on the furrows –
The million mouths of God.

In the morning,
In the cold grey morning,
Birds will break through these windows
And peck me up like corn.

Hannah

That kind of light again,
So white and hard it's like a blade
Slicing at my mind:
The car slips out of gear
Going up the long hill,
Then it's down the driveway,
The avenue of copper beech whispering
Over my head.

They walk like moving trees,
They're everywhere,
Hunched against no wind.

Leonard will be watching,
Up at the window in that stink
Of piss and disinfectant.
Watching.
He'll be pleased to see me:
Pleased at the new paper,
The paints, the stiff brush.

'Hannah's here, Leonard.'
As if he would say 'hello'
Or kiss me or do anything at all
But hang back in the shadows.
He'll show me his work,
Painting after painting,
All done since the last time:
Red shapes and black shapes,
And every one known to me,
Every one as if I'd painted it myself,
Long ago.

Here I am putting on the handbrake
And there he is,
Out of sight behind the tall pane,
And swirling between us, time,
Dangerous and glassy as a river.

Leonard

It's autumn in the red field,
The crows are blowing like dust,
Charcoal is specking a cold grey sky.
The furrows bend away like this,
You can feel it in your fingers,
In your warm heart:
A man is walking at the edge
Of the red field,
Walking away from me.

Some clouds:
The sun behind, saying
'Soon it will be cold,
I am behind the grey clouds.'

The bucket in the garden will freeze,
Sun will drop from the sky, from
Behind the clouds, saying
'I am gone from the clouds,
Gone from your window.'

The voices of crows
Will be happy in the red field,
Happy over the face of the man
Who has fallen,
Who I do not know
And have never known.

Hannah

What it meant was one cord,
One placenta:
Together everywhere,
On the very edge of everything together.
He was always there
And I was and always had been.

If he was taken away nothing fitted,
The loneliness swallowed me,
The nothingness, him not being there,
Until they put him back beside me
And it was myself returning.

We'd swum together all those months
Inside her, touching,
Caressing each other in the fluid
That buoyed our lives:
It must have been the closest thing.

Just echoes:
No words, no betrayal,
But that big heart pumping,
Booming in the fathoms of her life.

And us, drifting deeper and deeper
Into each other,
Until they lifted us towards the sky,
The first cry of separation.

Leonard

This is afternoon with Hannah:
We're in the big bed,
Traffic outside, sunshine
Dusty at the window.

The black cat is sleeping
Across us, soft and heavy;
It's hot, mother is downstairs,
Father is at work,
Not here at all.

The black cat is buzzing like a telephone:
This is the heat splashing,
Hotter and hotter.
The cat opens its eyes:
They're pieces of ice
Pulled from the garden bucket.

Hotter and hotter
And buzzing.
Hannah's hair is on fire in the sun,
A bluebottle climbs up the window
Into a spider's web:
It makes a noise like the wireless.
It goes on and on, shaking
The sky, breaking it into
White milky flakes.

I'm falling
Into the whiteness,
Into the hot flakes of snow.

Over here my father
Is the tallest man.
He is taller than the sun,
The clouds, the house,
Taller than my mother
With the biggest eyes and teeth
In the whole world:

Look, he is so tall that the red sun
Will burn him up to ash.

Hannah

We had been out all day
Playing in the wild fennel,
In the wide field, its smell
Minting our arms and legs.

When we came in she sat cradling
The teapot in her hands.
Nothing was ever so cold as that room
To our sun-dazed eyes,
Or ever so blank as that face
Which said over and over:
'Your daddy's dead,
Your daddy's dead.'
Her lips regular
As the hands of a clock,
Her mouth saying it:

Dead, dead,
Dead, dead.

One word measuring the loss,
Its dumbness entering Leonard
Like a stone.
He swallowed all that silence.
It lodged in his throat,
Choking him with the fear
That is still there,
As if he'd killed him
Or thought he had.

It happens every day,
In every town in every country
Of the world:
A man walks from the house
And never returns,
His chalk outline etched on the highway,
On the hearts from which he can never

Be erased:
He walked out under our spells,
Under out midnight curse
And never returned.

That night, huddled in bed,
The smell of fennel smothered us;
I knew he would never come back
To hold me, to touch me,
And the gladness flooded me
And the sorrow
Ate me.

My mother sobbed through darkness,
His footfalls still balanced in air
Outside our room,
And we waiting for them to fall
Upon the silence
Where that one word dripped
Like acid,
Corroding our young white bones.

Leonard

The flowers were buttery,
They made your hands all yellow,
They made the laughing come.

The grass was this high -
We were hidden,
Hidden in the sun,
In the smelling grass stalks.

This is the noise of grasshoppers,
Its grey smoke
Curling around us.

The goodness of the feeling
Is all yellow.
But the red field is still there,
With the tall man
Walking at the edge,
His hands on fire,
Reaching out for us.

It's the next field,
Or the field after that:
Never forget.

Hannah

It's all red now, everything red:
This is his bad time,
Red in the red field –
That damned field
I can't climb out of.

I tell him, 'Leonard
It can be any colour you choose.'
But I don't believe it.

I don't want to look anymore.
I take him outside onto the grass,
We pick up horse-chestnuts,
Smooth and brown and new,
Bursting from the green plush
Of their shells.

It's cool under the trees,
You can see scars where a branch
Came down in last year's gale.

Is he touching me because I'm crying?
It doesn't mean to say that I don't see you,
Because these tears are for us Leonard,
For us, for what happened,
Her not knowing what he did while she slept:
Our secret, our dumbness
Under the quilt in the hot bed.

I'm crying because tears
Are the colour of love,
And green is the coolness we long for,
The same shell,
The same deep cool shell.

Leonard

Hannah's face is pale, like
A winter sun falling;
A black bird flies straight across it.

I don't know the names of the birds.

Hannah will help me:
She'll pull the bird from her face
And maybe laugh, and say:

It's a so and so bird, Leonard –
She won't expect me to remember.

There should be clouds,
Blowing slowly like smoke,
Dark ones, with silver edges.

Soon the sun will be gone
From these windows:
Here is a moon coming from behind.

Shy at first, arriving too early,
Then bigger and bigger,
Tearing apart the black curtains
That cover the fields.

Hannah

If I was killed in the car
Or just died and didn't come,
What would it be like?

We started this together,
Side by side.

Or if he died and the telephone rang
To tell me.

Living with mother, her back
Bent like a question mark:
Hannah? Hannah?
And me, after all these years,
After this lifetime,
Not answering it right.

Her not knowing, holding on
To the memory of a man she never knew.
Was it because she didn't touch him
That we had to?
His sweat smell,
His sour breath hissing it:
'Touch me! Touch me!'
Sobbing, stroking our hair as we cried,
Terrified, telling us that he loved us,
That we were good children.

She tells me that I should have married.
And I want to say how I did,
How in the hot summer nights
I married a madman
Who loved me dumbly,
Who held me safe,
Who carried me out over the red field
And beyond,
Holding me, holding me

Under the light of the stars.

She won't come with me
And one day she'll die,
Curled in the bed,
Her cup of tea milky, separated by cold,
All these questions dammed behind her eyes,
Withering in her womb where
We made that first parting.

She held us inside herself,
Ran her hands over her blue-veined
Belly where we drifted in her waters:
Growing without light,
Touching like sea-drift.

I want to know what she thinks!
I want to shake her, to shout
'Mother, Mother. Tell me!'
But her eyes would just be blue,
The vaguest blue,
Insinuating themselves
Into the sky.

Leonard

It's today:
Today I like the tube paints best,
The metal shiny and heavy,
A good weight to squeeze
And see worms of paint squiggle out.

They gobble at the paper:
Sometimes I'm afraid of them.
Othertimes they're warm little flames
That won't harm me.

These trees are high and green:
It's a good morning for a blue car,
For the milkman's float.

The cleaner's mop goes round my feet
But I won't move.
The lady smiles and looks down this street.
She likes the street and the little man.

She can't see me hiding in the tall house.
Hiding at the window in the tall house,
Watching Hannah set off for school.

She can't see the dinner in her bag
That mother made, the carton of milk
And the green apple, so green
It was like a ball of ice.
But it's there.

I'm hiding
So Hannah won't look for me.
That way she can go and leave me
To the drawers and cupboards
And the shadow under the stairs
In the tall dark house
Where the tall dark man
Carries me away.

Hannah

Books, everyday these books!
Them and me, outstaring each other.
Stamping books, stacking books,
Sorting them, reading their black print
Which has so stained my heart.

My life is page after page –
A biography of other people's words
Sewn together in my mind.
A crazy lexicon, a patchwork,
Where words burn, more colours than words.
The stories more like threads
Stitching in and out of the days.

I take the books home for mother
And she reads them like a mole,
Tunnelling into them,
Escaping down their passageways of print.

And all the time, behind the high window,
Leonard is there, calling to me
Across the gravel path,
Across the cropped lawn,
The canopies of copper beech.

Our voices
Follow each other like waves,
Worry at the same shingle
Across the same long nights;
His cry is my echo,
His eyes wash over me through the glass,
Through the book covers,
Through the million words that drown me.

Leonard

You get the sound of leaves in your head
Like the touch of Hannah's hair,
Like the feel of being awake with her
In the moonlight in the wide bed.

There's the sound of a bird:
She will say it's an owl any minute.
Her eyes big like this,
Shining through the dark.

You get the clouds all streaky,
The moon, silver as a teapot,
And the brown humps of sleepers
Turning in the next room.

We're listening for footsteps
That we don't want to come:
The space between sounds is deep blue
And the holding each other is safe and green.

The sound of leaves is green too,
Like this whispering in Hannah's hair.
The sound of the birds
And the voice of the moon are silver.

In the bed it is orange,
Warm like flames, not cold
Like the high dark walls,
Like the windows looking back at me
Where footsteps tick tock
Backwards and forwards
And away.

Hannah

There's rain slicing at the windows today:
The pensioners come in
Shaking it from their gaberdines,
Mopping it from their old faces.
I'm thirty-three and feel like a child.

I think about myself,
What I am,
What made it like this:
One sperm rather than another.
The weather raging outside,
Taking them to bed.
A fateful conjunction of planets,
History poised on its fulcrum,
Overbalancing towards my future.

What would it be like to wear
Someone else's life, to
Have their soul in this flesh?

What chance was it that cursed Leonard
Or that blessed him?

I take books over the counter
Wipe rain from their covers.
The pensioners fuss and smile,
They stare at my ringless fingers,
Stare towards certain futures
And I feel the years draining away
Through every gutter in town.

When I'm alone at night
It grips me
Like a giant hand.
There's no thinking through it

Or past it,
Nothing but the gigantic sense
Of not being,
Of returning to before-birth blackness.

Not being:
A colossal loneliness, Leonard whimpering
In the wild fields of his imagination.
And I with nothing to comfort him,
Except my own fear.

Leonard

These are moonbeams coming down like bars
And these are the stars, like salt:
God is shaking them out over the emptiness.

It's like seeing through deep water,
Looking into the pond when ice lifted,
The cold scalding our hands.
Hannah held a piece to my cheek:
I laughed at the burning,
She made the cold feel warm.

The stars would be like that
If I could touch them.
I'd pick a basket of them
Or let Hannah choose
And lift them down for her
To wear in her ears.

This is high up, no fields can be seen,
Or farms or houses with lights.
It's looking upwards or lying down flat,
Feeling the whole world spin slowly,
Carrying us beyond the dark.

Hannah

Each day like the last, but added on.
Time is a chain of days dragging at my ankle.
Now mother can't move for the weight
Of links that bind her to the chair,
To the past.

What does she remember?

She's wasted all the words that might have helped,
She looks at me, helpless.
Does she remember the child that shared
Her womb with me?

Their sounds in the night,
Him gasping and her crying out,
Dragging me into waking –
Is he hurting her?
Hurting her?
Listening for his footsteps,
Feeling the weight of bedclothes
Like grave soil,
Sweat sticking me to the sheets,
Sleep settling again like an opaque
Grey shroud.

Then waking at last to touch Leonard,
To see his eyes flutter awake:
Outside, starlings quarrelling in the gutter,
Their slate eyes flicking against the light.

Leonard

Hannah is sad today:
Here eyes make the water
That runs down,
Grey sheets running down.

Her hands are birds
Touching here
Behind the rain.

The rest is all lines,
Grids,
Zig-zags, all jagged
Like the way the birds fly
Up to her face
And away into the rain.

Hannah makes the day like this.
She opens the gate to the red field
And I follow her in,
Wanting to touch her,
To keep her to myself.

Then I'm alone,
Alone in the red field
Rain hitting the lines of soil,
Mud squirting between my toes,
The birds flocking to Hannah's face.

And the sky is all grey,
Grey like this,
Over and over and over.

Hannah

At the funeral father was cremated,
The flames ate him in their red mouth.
We got the ashes later,
Took them home in a blue jar:
Everything was dust.

We scattered them in the fields
Behind our house,
Leonard wanting to hold the jar,
Rubbing it against himself
As if the genie of his father would grow
From its grey insides and spiral into life.

My mother's eyes were blank with light,
Unseethroughable, crazy mirrors:
She watched the dust fall from her hands,
Rubbing her wrists,
As if their blood had stopped.

Leonard had wanted to follow him in,
Wanted to pull the varnished oak man
Back from the flames.
'Daddy' was a word in a red mouth.
How could a man be a box?
How could a tree fall like a man?

He tore his hands on rose bushes outside,
Scattering their yellow petals,
Howling as if he knew there was no heaven
Or afterlife,
No redemption or salvation,
No hell but a heart still beating,
A love still glimmering, like bats,
Away into the dark.

Leonard

Hannah is asleep,
She is in the red field
Curled up like a mouse,
The wind chasing leaves over her.

I can't tell her about the field
Because wind is blowing me away.
These are the words:
The crows are pecking them up.

Hannah is afraid in the red field;
The sky is black all over.
She can't see father or mother
Even though they are waiting here
Near the grey river of ice.

I'm pulling at the gates,
Trying to reach her –
Remember it can be any colour.
If you lift up your hand
It can be any colour you choose.

I am in the red field,
Holding, trying to hold you down:
Close your mouth against the wind
Say my name over and over,
Hold me, remember.

Hannah

Every night
Needing him more and more:
Whatever colour it is
I want to be there with him,
I want to go back
To the frontier of what we are.

It's no use:
We're standing in the same field
With the same thin arms and legs,
The same mouths blackened by wind,
Those furrows zig-zagging
Like the jaws of traps,
Gnawing the sticks of our legs.

Wherever he is,
Needing him more and more
To go back with
To stand with
On the edge of everything;
To look through that same pane of ice
At the world shuddering,
In our hands.

No more waiting in the shadows
For me to come
Or for him to be there.
No more saying what it is
Or how we came to the border
With our hands held against the wind
And the birds spiralling away
With our words in their beaks.

Wherever he is I will stop saying it,
Let my fingers run over his name,
My tongue feel the rough edge of the days
And stay silent.

Whatever the sky,
The colour of the field,
Whatever the crop shivering
Under our lost feet.

Graham Mort

Graham Mort lives in North Yorkshire and works as a freelance writer, editor and creative-writing tutor. He has published four previous books of poetry and won a major Eric Gregory Award from the Society of Authors in 1985 for the poems in 'A Country on Fire'.

He has twice won a first prize in the Cheltenham Festival of Literature Poetry Competition and was awarded a Duncan Lawrie prize in the 1982 Arvon Foundation International Poetry Competition for his long poem 'A Halifax Cider Jar'; in 1992 his poem 'The Red Field' from this collection won the same prize.

He is currently the creative-writing Course Leader for the Open College of The Arts, where he has written and developed a number of correspondence writing courses, including specialised ones in poetry and short fiction. He has worked in many schools and colleges as a visiting writer and has specialised in designing and tutoring combined arts projects.

Graham Mort is an experienced performer of his work and has read to festival audiences and other groups throughout the country. His work has been broadcast on BBC radio and on television. In addition to poetry he writes short fiction and is a regular contributor of reviews and articles to literary and educational magazines.

Graham Mort   photo © Caroline Forbes